To Celebrate

____

____

Date

____

THANK YOU FOR COMING.

Let's celebrate!

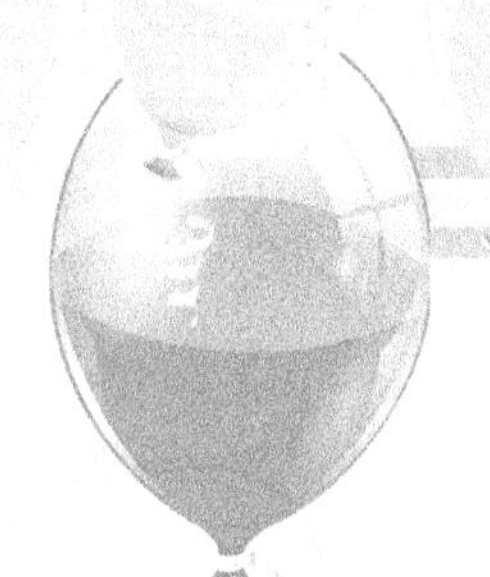

Guest Name

____

Wishes & Messages

____

____

____

____

____

____

EMAIL/PHONE
____

Guest Name

Wishes & Messages

Email/Phone

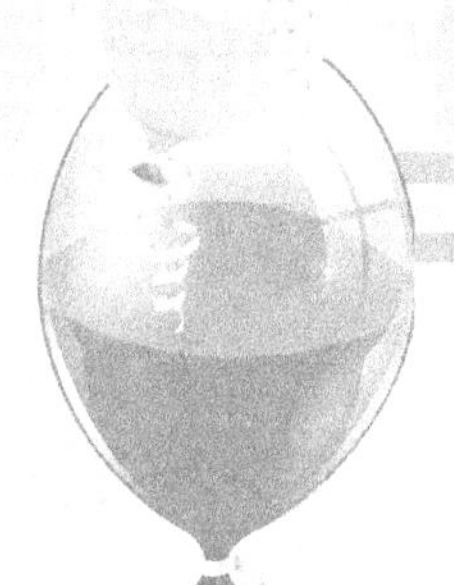

Guest Name

___

Wishes & Messages

___

___

___

___

___

___

___

Email/Phone
___

Wishes & Messages

Email/Phone

Guest Name

Wishes & Messages

Email/Phone

Guest Name

____

Wishes & Messages

____

____

____

____

____

____

Email/Phone _________________________________

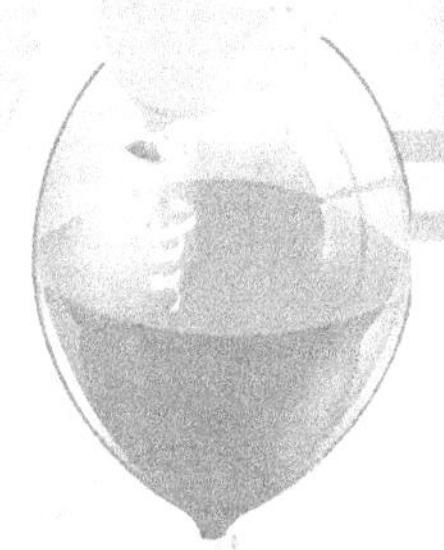

Guest Name

Wishes & Messages

Email/Phone

Guest Name

Wishes & Messages

Email/Phone

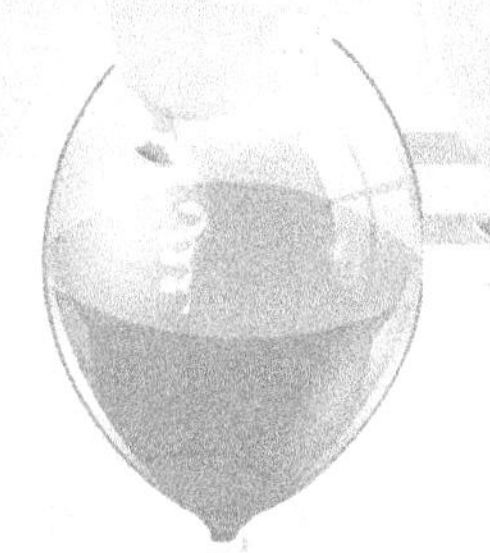

Guest Name

Wishes & Messages

Email/Phone

Guest Name

____

Wishes & Messages

____

____

____

____

____

____

Email/Phone _______________________________________

Guest Name

Wishes & Messages

Email/Phone

Guest Name

Wishes & Messages

Email/Phone

Guest Name

Wishes & Messages

Email/Phone

Guest Name

Wishes & Messages

Email/Phone

Guest Name

____

Wishes & Messages

____

____

____

____

____

____

Email/Phone
____

Guest Name

____

Wishes & Messages

____

____

____

____

____

____

Email/Phone
____

Guest Name

Wishes & Messages

Email/Phone

Guest Name

Wishes & Messages

Email/Phone

Guest Name

____

Wishes & Messages

____

____

____

____

____

____

Email/Phone _______________________________

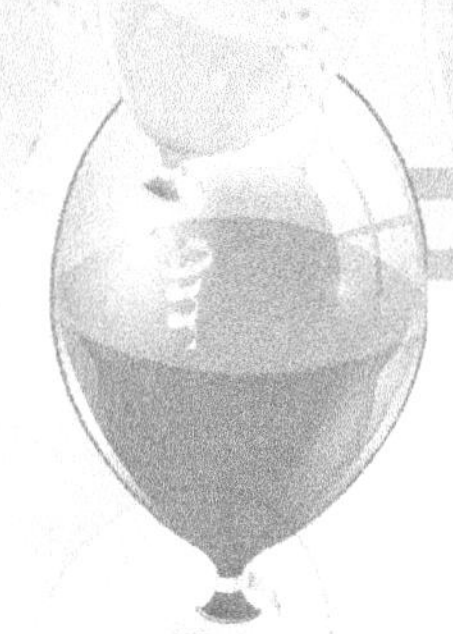

Guest Name

Wishes & Messages

Email/Phone

Guest Name

____

Wishes & Messages

____

____

____

____

____

____

Email/Phone
____

Guest Name

Wishes & Messages

Email/Phone

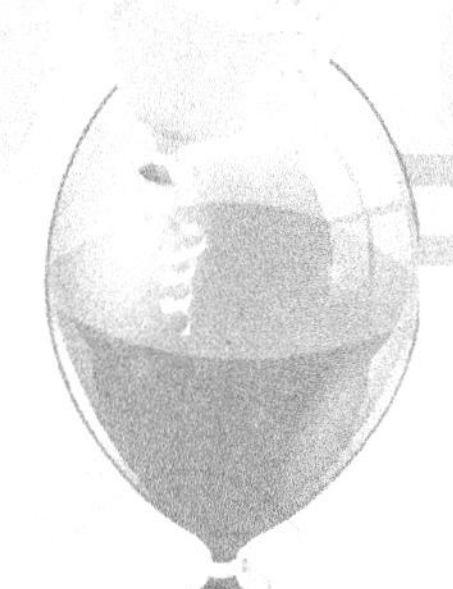

Guest Name

Wishes & Messages

Email/Phone

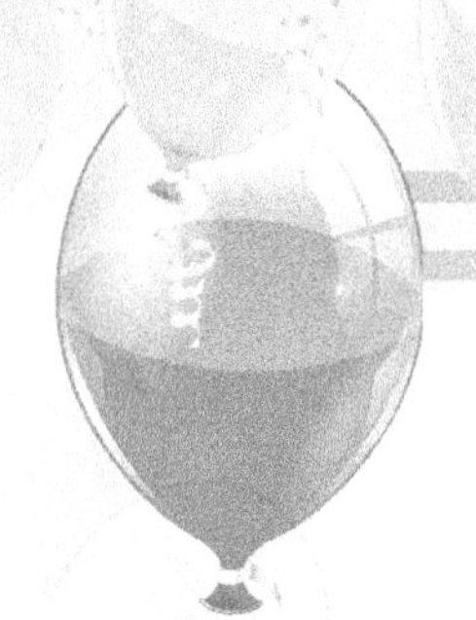

Guest Name

____

Wishes & Messages

____

____

____

____

____

____

____

Email/Phone
____

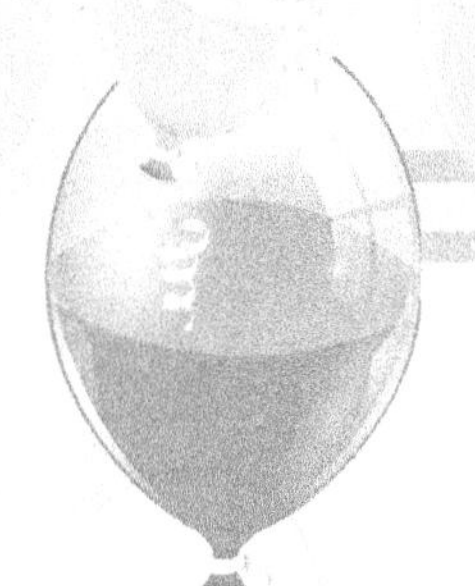

Guest Name

Wishes & Messages

Email/Phone

Guest Name

____

Wishes & Messages

____

____

____

____

____

____

____

Email/Phone _______________________________

Guest Name

Wishes & Messages

Email/Phone

Guest Name

____

Wishes & Messages

____

____

____

____

____

____

Email/Phone
____

Guest Name

Wishes & Messages

Email/Phone
____

Guest Name

____

Wishes & Messages

____

____

____

____

____

____

____

Email/Phone _______________________________________

Guest Name

Wishes & Messages

Email/Phone

Guest Name

____

Wishes & Messages

____

____

____

____

____

____

Email/Phone
____

Guest Name

Wishes & Messages

Email/Phone

Guest Name

Wishes & Messages

Email/Phone

Guest Name

Wishes & Messages

Email/Phone

Guest Name

____

Wishes & Messages

____

____

____

____

____

____

Email/Phone
____

Guest Name

Wishes & Messages

Email/Phone

Guest Name

Wishes & Messages

Email/Phone

Guest Name

Wishes & Messages

Email/Phone

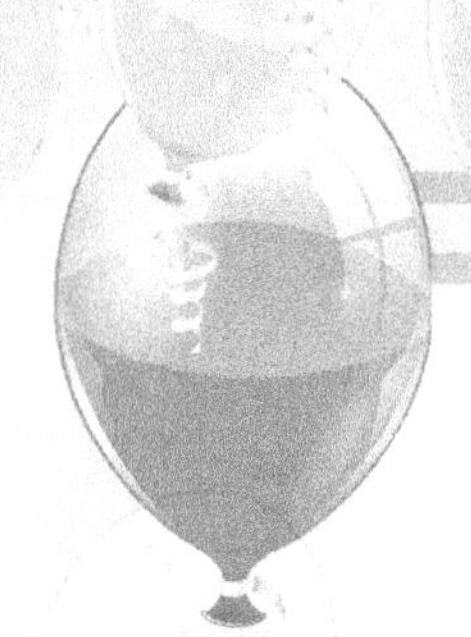

Guest Name

____

Wishes & Messages

____

____

____

____

____

____

____

Email/Phone

____

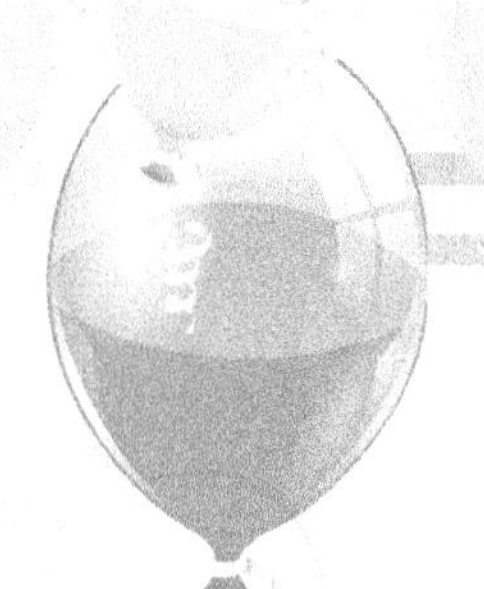

Guest Name

Wishes & Messages

Email/Phone

Guest Name

Wishes & Messages

Email/Phone

Guest Name

____

Wishes & Messages

____

____

____

____

____

____

____

Email/Phone
____

Guest Name

____

Wishes & Messages

____

____

____

____

____

____

Email/Phone
____

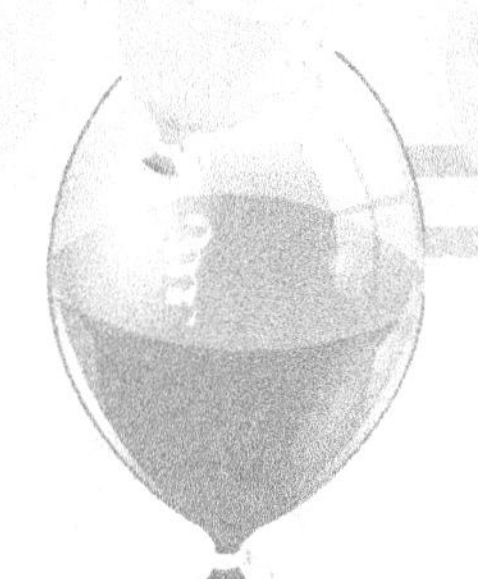

Guest Name

Wishes & Messages

Email/Phone

Guest Name

Wishes & Messages

Email/Phone

Guest Name

___

Wishes & Messages

___

___

___

___

___

___

___

Email/Phone
___

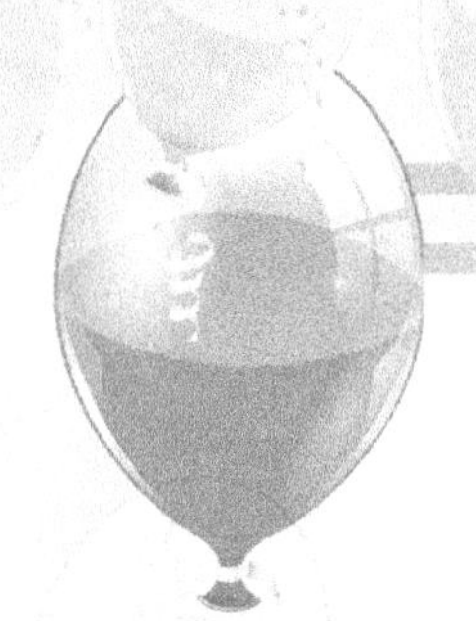

Guest Name

Wishes & Messages

Email/Phone

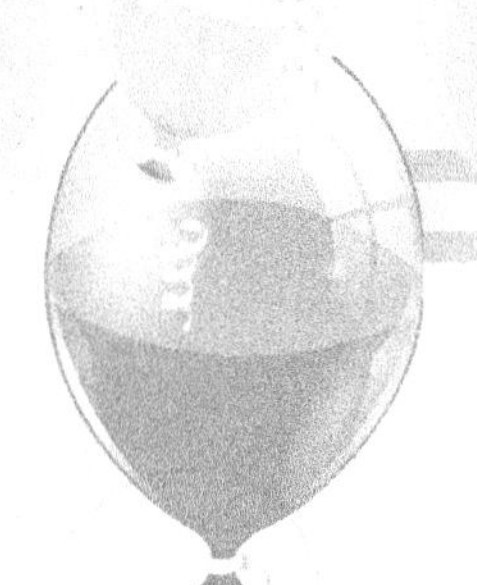

Guest Name

Wishes & Messages

Email/Phone

Guest Name

Wishes & Messages

Email/Phone

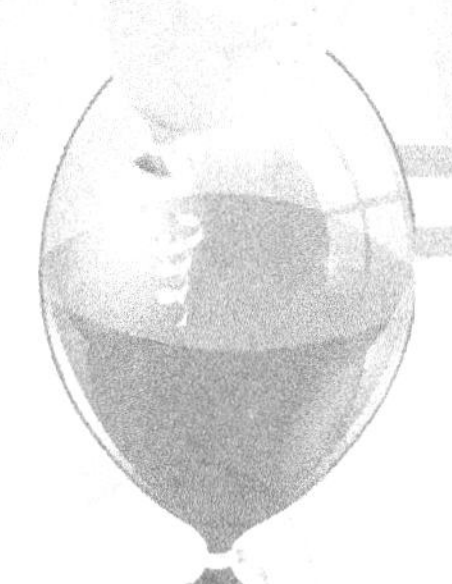

Guest Name

Wishes & Messages

Email/Phone

Guest Name

____

Wishes & Messages

____

____

____

____

____

____

____

Email/Phone
____

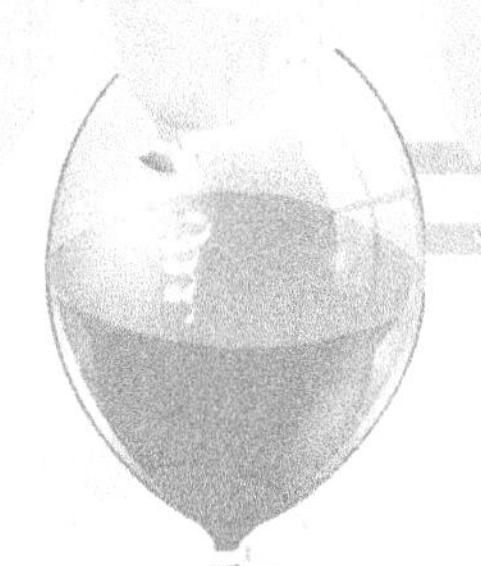

Guest Name

____

Wishes & Messages

____

____

____

____

____

____

Email/Phone

____

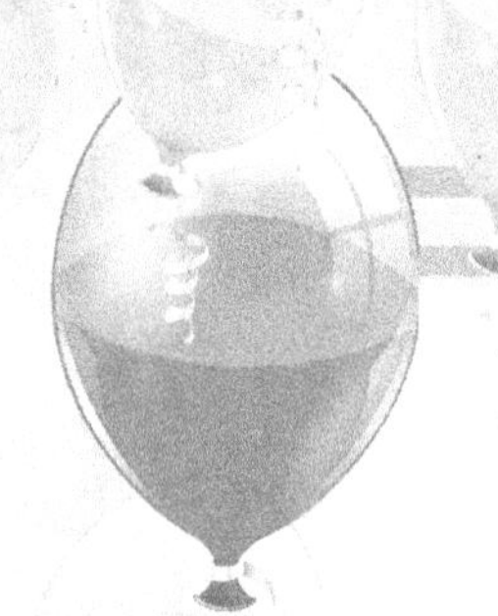

Guest Name

____

Wishes & Messages

____

____

____

____

____

____

____

Email/Phone
____

Guest Name

Wishes & Messages

Email/Phone

Guest Name

Wishes & Messages

Email/Phone

Guest Name

Wishes & Messages

Email/Phone

Guest Name

Wishes & Messages

Email/Phone

Guest Name

Wishes & Messages

Email/Phone

Guest Name

Wishes & Messages

Email/Phone

Guest Name

Wishes & Messages

Email/Phone

Guest Name

Wishes & Messages

Email/Phone

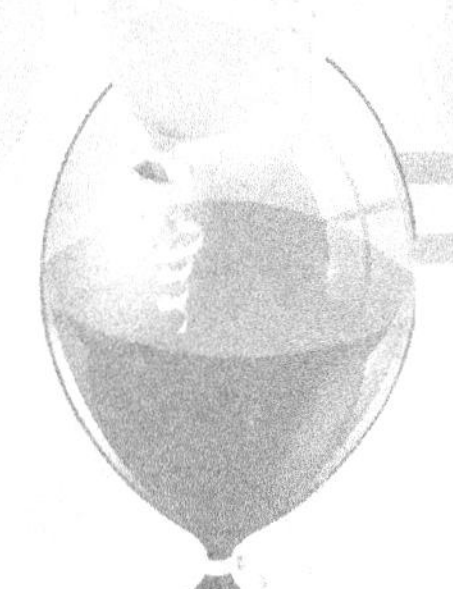

Guest Name

Wishes & Messages

Email/Phone

Guest Name

____

Wishes & Messages

____

____

____

____

____

____

Email/Phone _______________________

Guest Name

____

Wishes & Messages

____

____

____

____

____

____

Email/Phone
____

Guest Name

Wishes & Messages

Email/Phone

Guest Name

Wishes & Messages

____

____

____

____

____

____

Email/Phone
____

Guest Name

Wishes & Messages

EMAIL/PHONE

Guest Name

Wishes & Messages

Email/Phone

Guest Name

Wishes & Messages

Email/Phone
____

Guest Name

Wishes & Messages

Email/Phone

Guest Name

Wishes & Messages

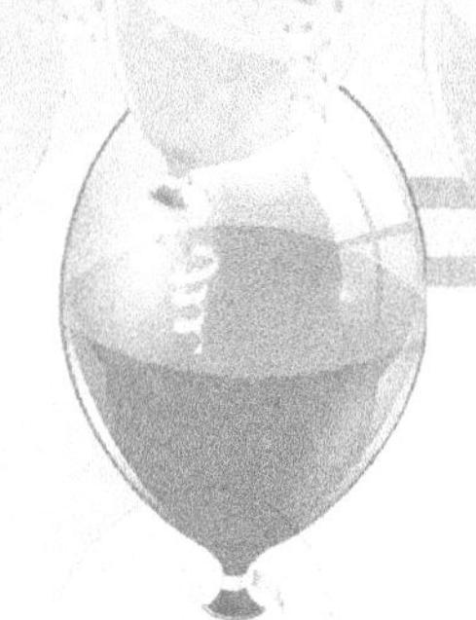

Email/Phone

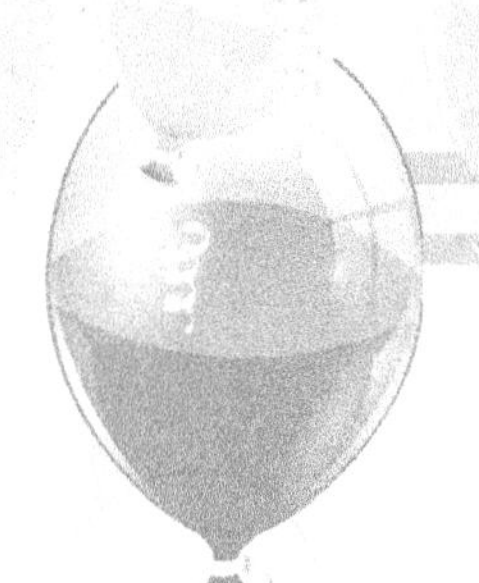

Guest Name

Wishes & Messages

Email/Phone
____

Guest Name

Wishes & Messages

Email/Phone

Guest Name

Wishes & Messages

Email/Phone

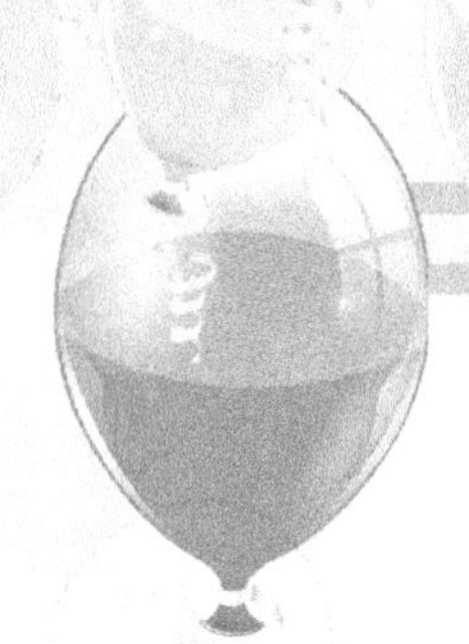

Guest Name

____

Wishes & Messages

____

____

____

____

____

____

Email/Phone
____

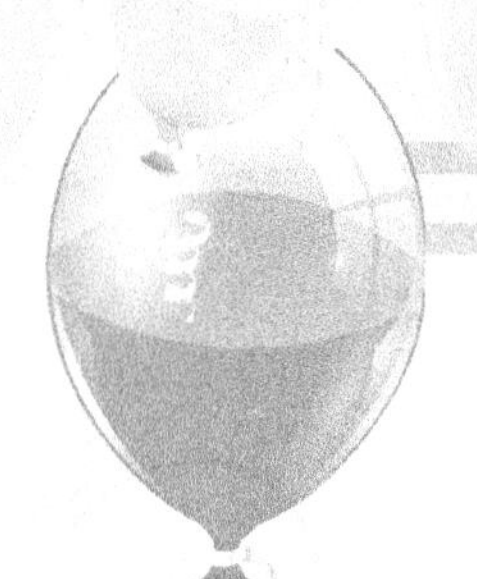

Guest Name

Wishes & Messages

Email/Phone

Guest Name

____

Wishes & Messages

____

____

____

____

____

____

____

Email/Phone
____

Guest Name

Wishes & Messages

Email/Phone

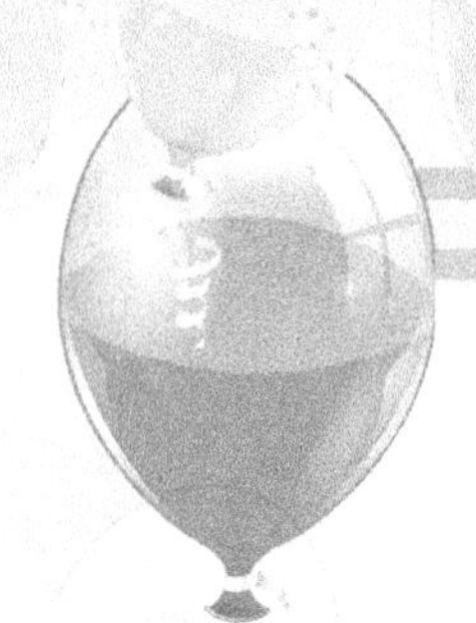

Guest Name

____

Wishes & Messages

____

____

____

____

____

____

Email/Phone
____

Guest Name

Wishes & Messages

Email/Phone

Guest Name

Wishes & Messages

Email/Phone

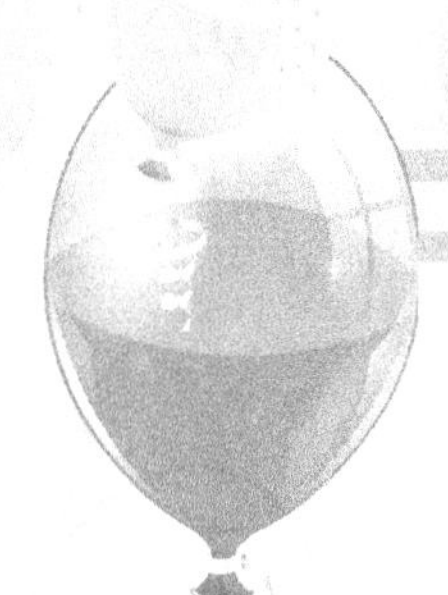

Guest Name

Wishes & Messages

Email/Phone

Guest Name

____

Wishes & Messages

____

____

____

____

____

____

Email/Phone _________________________________

Guest Name

Wishes & Messages

Email/Phone

Guest Name

Wishes & Messages

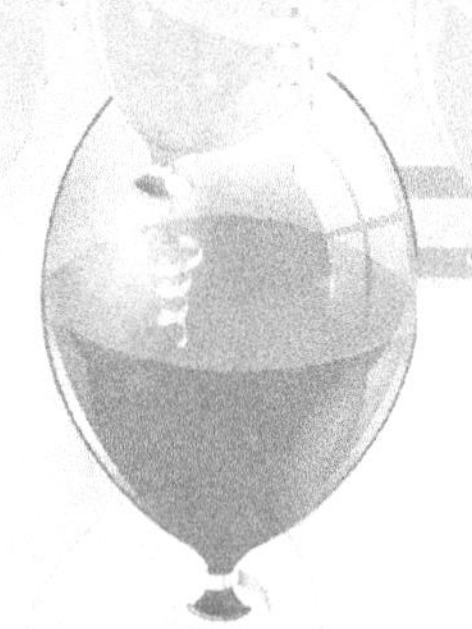

Email/Phone

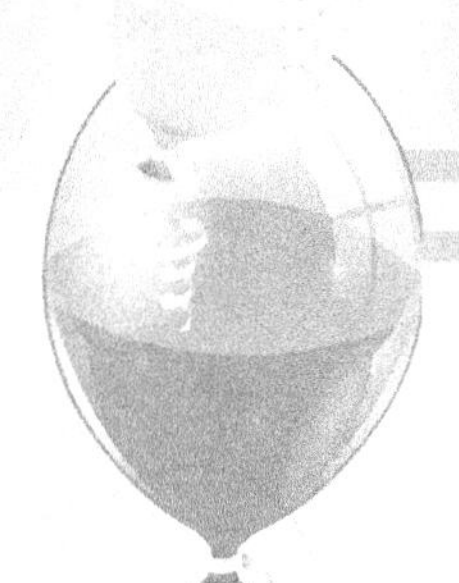

Guest Name

Wishes & Messages

Email/Phone

Guest Name

Wishes & Messages

Email/Phone

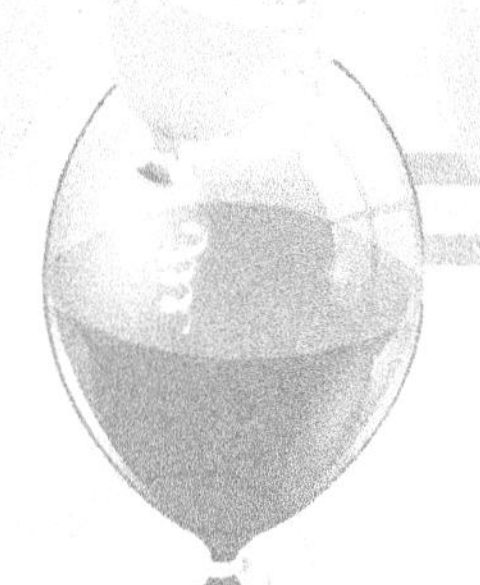

Guest Name

Wishes & Messages

Email/Phone

Guest Name

Wishes & Messages

Email/Phone

Guest Name

Wishes & Messages

Email/Phone

Guest Name

Wishes & Messages

Email/Phone

Guest Name

Wishes & Messages

Email/Phone

Guest Name

Wishes & Messages

Email/Phone

Guest Name

Wishes & Messages

Email/Phone

Guest Name

Wishes & Messages

Email/Phone

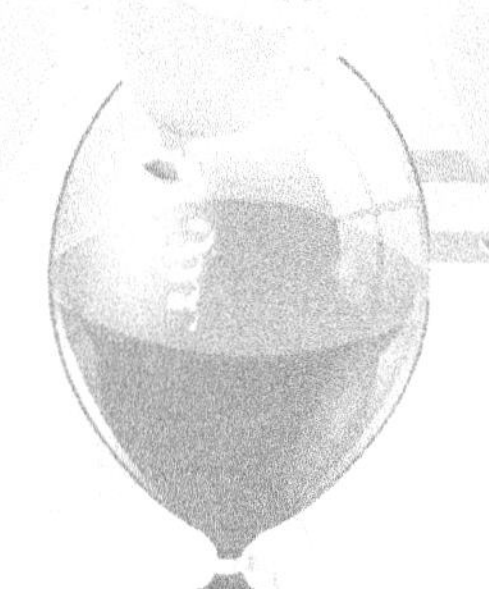

Guest Name

Wishes & Messages

Email/Phone

Guest Name

Wishes & Messages

Email/Phone

Guest Name

Wishes & Messages

Email/Phone

Guest Name

Wishes & Messages

Email/Phone

Guest Name

Wishes & Messages

Email/Phone

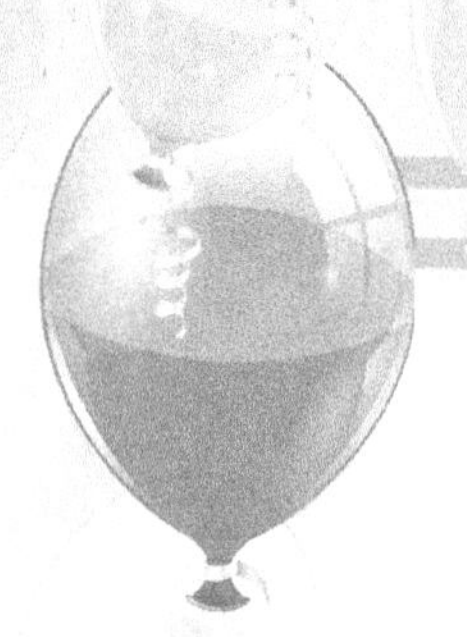

Guest Name

____

Wishes & Messages

____

____

____

____

____

____

____

Email/Phone
____

Guest Name

Wishes & Messages

Email/Phone

Guest Name

Wishes & Messages

Email/Phone

Guest Name

____

Wishes & Messages

____

____

____

____

____

____

EMAIL/PHONE
____

Guest Name

____

Wishes & Messages

____

____

____

____

____

____

____

Email/Phone ___________________________

NOTES & PHOTOS

NOTES & PHOTOS

NOTES & PHOTOS

NOTES & PHOTOS

NOTES & PHOTOS

GIFT LOG

Name / Email / Phone | *Gift*

GIFT LOG

Name / Email / Phone	Gift

GIFT LOG

Name /Email /Phone	Gift

GIFT LOG

Name / Email / Phone	Gift

GIFT LOG

Name / Email / Phone	Gift

GIFT LOG

Name / Email / Phone   Gift

GIFT LOG

Name / Email / Phone   Gift